Date _____

Location _____

Sermon Title _____

Who's Preaching _____

Scripture _____

Word(s) To Look Up/Remember

_____

_____

Sermon Notes

_____

_____

_____

_____

_____

_____

_____

_____

_____

_____

_____

_____

_____

_____

_____

_____

_____

_____

_____

_____

_____

_____

_____

_____

_____

_____

_____

_____

_____

_____

Today's sermon encourages me to:

_____

_____

_____

A quote, saying I want to share:

_____

_____

_____

The Word of God - Amen

Date _____

Location _____

Sermon Title _____

Who's Preaching _____

Scripture _____

Word(s) To Look Up/Remember

_____

_____

Sermon Notes

_____

_____

_____

_____

_____

_____

_____

_____

_____

_____

_____

_____

_____

_____

_____

_____

_____

_____

_____

_____

_____

_____

_____

_____

_____

_____

_____

_____

_____

Today's sermon encourages me to:

_____

_____

_____

_____

A quote,saying I want to share:

_____

_____

_____

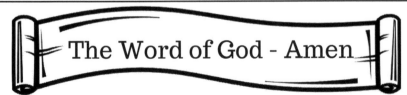
The Word of God - Amen

Date _____

Location _____

Sermon Title _____

Who's Preaching _____

Scripture _____

Word(s) To Look Up/Remember

_____

_____

Sermon Notes

_____

_____

_____

_____

_____

_____

_____

_____

_____

_____

_____

_____

_____

_____

_____

_____

_____

_____

_____

_____

_____

_____

_____

_____

_____

_____

_____

_____

Today's sermon encourages me to:

_____

_____

_____

A quote,saying I want to share:

_____

_____

_____

The Word of God - Amen

Date _____

Location _____

Sermon Title _____

Who's Preaching _____

Scripture _____

Word(s) To Look Up/Remember

_____

_____

Sermon Notes

_____

_____

_____

_____

_____

_____

_____

_____

_____

_____

_____

_____

_____

_____

_____

_____

_____

_____

_____

_____

_____

_____

_____

_____

_____

_____

_____

_____

_____

Today's sermon encourages me to:

_____

_____

_____

A quote,saying I want to share:

_____

_____

_____

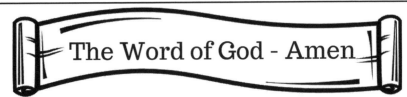
The Word of God - Amen

Date _____

Location _____

Sermon Title _____

Who's Preaching _____

Scripture _____

Word(s) To Look Up/Remember

_____

_____

Sermon Notes

_____

_____

_____

_____

_____

_____

_____

_____

_____

_____

_____

_____

_____

_____

_____

_____

_____

_____

_____

_____

_____

_____

_____

_____

_____

_____

_____

_____

_____

_____

Today's sermon encourages me to:

_____

_____

_____

_____

A quote,saying I want to share:

_____

_____

_____

The Word of God - Amen

Date _____

Location _____

Sermon Title _____

Who's Preaching _____

Scripture _____

Word(s) To Look Up/Remember

_____

_____

Sermon Notes

_____

_____

_____

_____

_____

_____

_____

_____

_____

_____

_____

_____

_____

_____

_____

_____

_____

_____

_____

_____

_____

_____

_____

_____

_____

_____

_____

Today's sermon encourages me to:

_____

_____

_____

A quote,saying I want to share:

_____

_____

_____

The Word of God - Amen

Date _____

Location _____

Sermon Title _____

Who's Preaching _____

Scripture _____

Word(s) To Look Up/Remember

_____

_____

Sermon Notes

_____

_____

_____

_____

_____

_____

_____

_____

_____

_____

_____

_____

_____

_____

_____

_____

_____

_____

_____

_____

_____

_____

_____

_____

_____

_____

_____

_____

_____

_____

Today's sermon encourages me to:

_____

_____

_____

_____

A quote,saying I want to share:

_____

_____

_____

The Word of God - Amen

Date _____

Location _____

Sermon Title _____

Who's Preaching _____

Scripture _____

Word(s) To Look Up/Remember

_____

_____

Sermon Notes

_____

_____

_____

_____

_____

_____

_____

_____

_____

_____

_____

_____

_____

_____

_____

_____

_____

_____

_____

_____

_____

_____

_____

_____

_____

_____

_____

_____

_____

Today's sermon encourages me to:

_____

_____

_____

A quote,saying I want to share:

_____

_____

_____

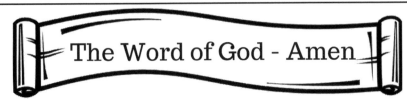
The Word of God - Amen

Date _____

Location _____

Sermon Title _____

Who's Preaching _____

Scripture _____

Word(s) To Look Up/Remember

_____

_____

Sermon Notes

_____

_____

_____

_____

_____

_____

_____

_____

_____

_____

_____

_____

_____

_____

_____

_____

_____

_____

_____

_____

_____

_____

_____

_____

_____

_____

_____

_____

_____

Today's sermon encourages me to:

_____

_____

_____

A quote,saying I want to share:

_____

_____

_____

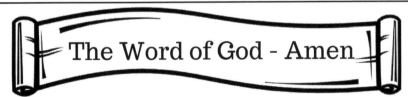

The Word of God - Amen

Date _____

Location _____

Sermon Title _____

Who's Preaching _____

Scripture _____

Word(s) To Look Up/Remember

_____

_____

Sermon Notes

_____

_____

_____

_____

_____

_____

_____

_____

_____

_____

_____

_____

_____

_____

_____

_____

_____

_____

_____

_____

_____

_____

_____

_____

_____

_____

_____

_____

_____

Today's sermon encourages me to:

_____

_____

_____

_____

A quote,saying I want to share:

_____

_____

_____

The Word of God - Amen

Date _____

Location _____

Sermon Title _____

Who's Preaching _____

Scripture _____

Word(s) To Look Up/Remember

_____

_____

Sermon Notes

_____

_____

_____

_____

_____

_____

_____

_____

_____

_____

_____

_____

_____

_____

_____

_____

_____

_____

_____

_____

_____

_____

_____

_____

_____

_____

_____

Today's sermon encourages me to:

_____

_____

_____

A quote,saying I want to share:

_____

_____

_____

The Word of God - Amen

Date _____

Location _____

Sermon Title _____

Who's Preaching _____

Scripture _____

Word(s) To Look Up/Remember

_____

_____

Sermon Notes

_____

_____

_____

_____

_____

_____

_____

_____

_____

_____

_____

_____

_____

_____

_____

_____

_____

_____

_____

_____

_____

_____

_____

_____

_____

_____

Today's sermon encourages me to:

_____

_____

_____

A quote,saying I want to share:

_____

_____

_____

The Word of God - Amen

Date _____

Location _____

Sermon Title _____

Who's Preaching _____

Scripture _____

Word(s) To Look Up/Remember

_____

_____

Sermon Notes

_____

_____

_____

_____

_____

_____

_____

_____

_____

_____

_____

_____

_____

_____

_____

_____

_____

_____

_____

_____

_____

_____

_____

_____

_____

_____

_____

_____

Today's sermon encourages me to:

_____

_____

_____

A quote, saying I want to share:

_____

_____

_____

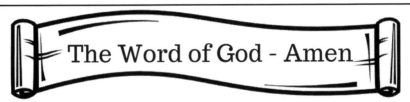
The Word of God - Amen

Date _____

Location _____

Sermon Title _____

Who's Preaching _____

Scripture _____

Word(s) To Look Up/Remember

_____

_____

Sermon Notes

_____

_____

_____

_____

_____

_____

_____

_____

_____

_____

_____

_____

_____

_____

_____

_____

_____

_____

_____

_____

_____

_____

_____

_____

_____

_____

_____

_____

Today's sermon encourages me to:

_____

_____

_____

A quote,saying I want to share:

_____

_____

_____

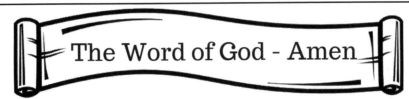

The Word of God - Amen

Date _____

Location _____

Sermon Title _____

Who's Preaching _____

Scripture _____

Word(s) To Look Up/Remember

_____

_____

Sermon Notes

_____

_____

_____

_____

_____

_____

_____

_____

_____

_____

_____

_____

_____

_____

_____

_____

_____

_____

_____

_____

_____

_____

_____

_____

_____

_____

_____

Today's sermon encourages me to:

_____

_____

_____

A quote,saying I want to share:

_____

_____

_____

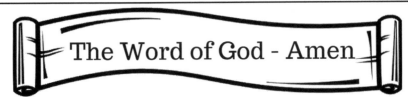

The Word of God - Amen

Date _____

Location _____

Sermon Title _____

Who's Preaching _____

Scripture _____

Word(s) To Look Up/Remember

_____

_____

Sermon Notes

_____

_____

_____

_____

_____

_____

_____

_____

_____

_____

_____

_____

_____

_____

_____

_____

_____

_____

_____

_____

_____

_____

_____

_____

_____

_____

_____

_____

Today's sermon encourages me to:

_____

_____

_____

_____

A quote,saying I want to share:

_____

_____

_____

The Word of God - Amen

Date _____

Location _____

Sermon Title _____

Who's Preaching _____

Scripture _____

Word(s) To Look Up/Remember

_____

_____

Sermon Notes

_____

_____

_____

_____

_____

_____

_____

_____

_____

_____

_____

_____

_____

_____

_____

_____

_____

_____

_____

_____

_____

_____

_____

_____

_____

_____

Today's sermon encourages me to:

_____

_____

_____

A quote,saying I want to share:

_____

_____

_____

The Word of God - Amen

Date _____

Location _____

Sermon Title _____

Who's Preaching _____

Scripture _____

Word(s) To Look Up/Remember

_____

_____

Sermon Notes

_____

_____

_____

_____

_____

_____

_____

_____

_____

_____

_____

_____

_____

_____

_____

_____

_____

_____

_____

_____

_____

_____

_____

_____

_____

_____

_____

_____

Today's sermon encourages me to:

_____

_____

_____

A quote,saying I want to share:

_____

_____

_____

The Word of God - Amen

Date _____

Location _____

Sermon Title _____

Who's Preaching _____

Scripture _____

Word(s) To Look Up/Remember

_____

_____

Sermon Notes

_____

_____

_____

_____

_____

_____

_____

_____

_____

_____

_____

_____

_____

_____

_____

_____

_____

_____

_____

_____

_____

_____

_____

_____

_____

_____

_____

Today's sermon encourages me to:

_____

_____

_____

_____

A quote,saying I want to share:

_____

_____

_____

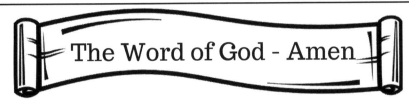

The Word of God - Amen

Date _____

Location _____

Sermon Title _____

Who's Preaching _____

Scripture _____

Word(s) To Look Up/Remember

_____

_____

Sermon Notes

_____

_____

_____

_____

_____

_____

_____

_____

_____

_____

_____

_____

_____

_____

_____

_____

_____

_____

_____

_____

_____

_____

_____

_____

_____

_____

_____

Today's sermon encourages me to:

_____

_____

_____

A quote,saying I want to share:

_____

_____

_____

The Word of God - Amen

Date _____

Location _____

Sermon Title _____

Who's Preaching _____

Scripture _____

Word(s) To Look Up/Remember

_____

_____

Sermon Notes

_____

_____

_____

_____

_____

_____

_____

_____

_____

_____

_____

_____

_____

_____

_____

_____

_____

_____

_____

_____

_____

_____

_____

_____

_____

_____

_____

_____

Today's sermon encourages me to:

_____

_____

_____

A quote,saying I want to share:

_____

_____

_____

The Word of God - Amen

Date _____

Location _____

Sermon Title _____

Who's Preaching _____

Scripture _____

Word(s) To Look Up/Remember

_____

_____

Sermon Notes

_____

_____

_____

_____

_____

_____

_____

_____

_____

_____

_____

_____

_____

_____

_____

_____

_____

_____

_____

_____

_____

_____

_____

_____

_____

_____

Today's sermon encourages me to:

_____

_____

_____

A quote, saying I want to share:

_____

_____

_____

The Word of God - Amen

Date _____

Location _____

Sermon Title _____

Who's Preaching _____

Scripture _____

Word(s) To Look Up/Remember

_____

_____

Sermon Notes

_____

_____

_____

_____

_____

_____

_____

_____

_____

_____

_____

_____

_____

_____

_____

_____

_____

_____

_____

_____

_____

_____

_____

_____

_____

_____

Today's sermon encourages me to:

_____

_____

_____

A quote,saying I want to share:

_____

_____

_____

The Word of God - Amen

Date _____

Location _____

Sermon Title _____

Who's Preaching _____

Scripture _____

Word(s) To Look Up/Remember

_____

_____

Sermon Notes

_____

_____

_____

_____

_____

_____

_____

_____

_____

_____

_____

_____

_____

_____

_____

_____

_____

_____

_____

_____

_____

_____

_____

_____

_____

_____

_____

Today's sermon encourages me to:

_____

_____

_____

_____

A quote,saying I want to share:

_____

_____

_____

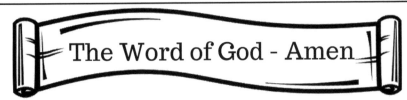

The Word of God - Amen

Date _____

Location _____

Sermon Title _____

Who's Preaching _____

Scripture _____

Word(s) To Look Up/Remember

_____

_____

Sermon Notes

_____

_____

_____

_____

_____

_____

_____

_____

_____

_____

_____

_____

_____

_____

_____

_____

_____

_____

_____

_____

_____

_____

_____

_____

_____

_____

_____

Today's sermon encourages me to:

_____

_____

_____

A quote,saying I want to share:

_____

_____

_____

The Word of God - Amen

Date _____

Location _____

Sermon Title _____

Who's Preaching _____

Scripture _____

Word(s) To Look Up/Remember

_____

_____

Sermon Notes

_____

_____

_____

_____

_____

_____

_____

_____

_____

_____

_____

_____

_____

_____

_____

_____

_____

_____

_____

_____

_____

_____

_____

_____

_____

_____

_____

_____

_____

Today's sermon encourages me to:

_____

_____

_____

_____

A quote,saying I want to share:

_____

_____

_____

The Word of God - Amen

Date _____

Location _____

Sermon Title _____

Who's Preaching _____

Scripture _____

Word(s) To Look Up/Remember

_____

_____

Sermon Notes

_____

_____

_____

_____

_____

_____

_____

_____

_____

_____

_____

_____

_____

_____

_____

_____

_____

_____

_____

_____

_____

_____

_____

_____

_____

_____

_____

_____

Today's sermon encourages me to:

_____

_____

_____

A quote,saying I want to share:

_____

_____

_____

The Word of God - Amen

Date _____

Location _____

Sermon Title _____

Who's Preaching _____

Scripture _____

Word(s) To Look Up/Remember

_____

_____

Sermon Notes

_____

_____

_____

_____

_____

_____

_____

_____

_____

_____

_____

_____

_____

_____

_____

_____

_____

_____

_____

_____

_____

_____

_____

_____

_____

_____

_____

_____

_____

Today's sermon encourages me to:

_____

_____

_____

_____

A quote,saying I want to share:

_____

_____

_____

The Word of God - Amen

Date _____

Location _____

Sermon Title _____

Who's Preaching _____

Scripture _____

Word(s) To Look Up/Remember

_____

_____

Sermon Notes

_____

_____

_____

_____

_____

_____

_____

_____

_____

_____

_____

_____

_____

_____

_____

_____

_____

_____

_____

_____

_____

_____

_____

_____

_____

_____

_____

_____

Today's sermon encourages me to:

_____

_____

_____

_____

A quote, saying I want to share:

_____

_____

_____

The Word of God - Amen

Date _____

Location _____

Sermon Title _____

Who's Preaching _____

Scripture _____

Word(s) To Look Up/Remember

_____

_____

Sermon Notes

_____

_____

_____

_____

_____

_____

_____

_____

_____

_____

_____

_____

_____

_____

_____

_____

_____

_____

_____

_____

_____

_____

_____

_____

_____

_____

_____

Today's sermon encourages me to:

_____

_____

_____

A quote,saying I want to share:

_____

_____

_____

The Word of God - Amen

Date _____

Location _____

Sermon Title _____

Who's Preaching _____

Scripture _____

Word(s) To Look Up/Remember

_____

_____

Sermon Notes

_____

_____

_____

_____

_____

_____

_____

_____

_____

_____

_____

_____

_____

_____

_____

_____

_____

_____

_____

_____

_____

_____

_____

_____

_____

_____

_____

_____

Today's sermon encourages me to:

_____

_____

_____

_____

A quote,saying I want to share:

_____

_____

_____

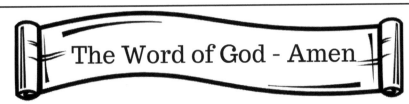

The Word of God - Amen

Date _____

Location _____

Sermon Title _____

Who's Preaching _____

Scripture _____

Word(s) To Look Up/Remember

_____

_____

Sermon Notes

_____

_____

_____

_____

_____

_____

_____

_____

_____

_____

_____

_____

_____

_____

_____

_____

_____

_____

_____

_____

_____

_____

_____

_____

_____

_____

_____

_____

_____

Today's sermon encourages me to:

_____

_____

_____

_____

A quote, saying I want to share:

_____

_____

_____

The Word of God - Amen

Date _____

Location _____

Sermon Title _____

Who's Preaching _____

Scripture _____

Word(s) To Look Up/Remember

_____

_____

Sermon Notes

_____

_____

_____

_____

_____

_____

_____

_____

_____

_____

_____

_____

_____

_____

_____

_____

_____

_____

_____

_____

_____

_____

_____

_____

_____

_____

_____

Today's sermon encourages me to:

_____

_____

_____

_____

A quote,saying I want to share:

_____

_____

_____

The Word of God - Amen

Date _____

Location _____

Sermon Title _____

Who's Preaching _____

Scripture _____

Word(s) To Look Up/Remember

_____

_____

Sermon Notes

_____

_____

_____

_____

_____

_____

_____

_____

_____

_____

_____

_____

_____

_____

_____

_____

_____

_____

_____

_____

_____

_____

_____

_____

_____

_____

_____

_____

_____

Today's sermon encourages me to:

_____

_____

_____

_____

A quote,saying I want to share:

_____

_____

_____

The Word of God - Amen

Date _____

Location _____

Sermon Title _____

Who's Preaching _____

Scripture _____

Word(s) To Look Up/Remember

_____

_____

Sermon Notes

_____

_____

_____

_____

_____

_____

_____

_____

_____

_____

_____

_____

_____

_____

_____

_____

_____

_____

_____

_____

_____

_____

_____

_____

_____

_____

_____

_____

Today's sermon encourages me to:

_____

_____

_____

_____

A quote,saying I want to share:

_____

_____

_____

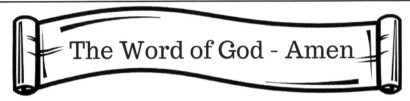

The Word of God - Amen

Date _____

Location _____

Sermon Title _____

Who's Preaching _____

Scripture _____

Word(s) To Look Up/Remember

_____

_____

Sermon Notes

_____

_____

_____

_____

_____

_____

_____

_____

_____

_____

_____

_____

_____

_____

_____

_____

_____

_____

_____

_____

_____

_____

_____

_____

_____

_____

_____

Today's sermon encourages me to:

_____

_____

_____

_____

A quote,saying I want to share:

_____

_____

_____

The Word of God - Amen

Date _____

Location _____

Sermon Title _____

Who's Preaching _____

Scripture _____

Word(s) To Look Up/Remember

_____

_____

Sermon Notes

_____

_____

_____

_____

_____

_____

_____

_____

_____

_____

_____

_____

_____

_____

_____

_____

_____

_____

_____

_____

_____

_____

_____

_____

_____

_____

_____

_____

Today's sermon encourages me to:

_____

_____

_____

A quote,saying I want to share:

_____

_____

_____

The Word of God - Amen

Date _____

Location _____

Sermon Title _____

Who's Preaching _____

Scripture _____

Word(s) To Look Up/Remember

_____

_____

Sermon Notes

_____

_____

_____

_____

_____

_____

_____

_____

_____

_____

_____

_____

_____

_____

_____

_____

_____

_____

_____

_____

_____

_____

_____

_____

_____

_____

Today's sermon encourages me to:

_____

_____

_____

A quote,saying I want to share:

_____

_____

_____

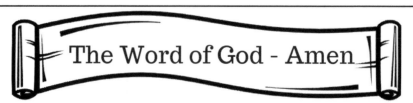

The Word of God - Amen

Date _____

Location _____

Sermon Title _____

Who's Preaching _____

Scripture _____

Word(s) To Look Up/Remember

_____

_____

Sermon Notes

_____

_____

_____

_____

_____

_____

_____

_____

_____

_____

_____

_____

_____

_____

_____

_____

_____

_____

_____

_____

_____

_____

_____

_____

_____

_____

_____

_____

_____

Today's sermon encourages me to:

_____

_____

_____

_____

A quote,saying I want to share:

_____

_____

_____

The Word of God - Amen

Date _____

Location _____

Sermon Title _____

Who's Preaching _____

Scripture _____

Word(s) To Look Up/Remember

_____

_____

Sermon Notes

_____

_____

_____

_____

_____

_____

_____

_____

_____

_____

_____

_____

_____

_____

_____

_____

_____

_____

_____

_____

_____

_____

_____

_____

_____

_____

_____

_____

_____

_____

Today's sermon encourages me to:

_____

_____

_____

_____

A quote,saying I want to share:

_____

_____

_____

The Word of God - Amen

Date _____

Location _____

Sermon Title _____

Who's Preaching _____

Scripture _____

Word(s) To Look Up/Remember

_____

_____

Sermon Notes

_____

_____

_____

_____

_____

_____

_____

_____

_____

_____

_____

_____

_____

_____

_____

_____

_____

_____

_____

_____

_____

_____

_____

_____

_____

_____

_____

_____

_____

Today's sermon encourages me to:

_____

_____

_____

_____

A quote, saying I want to share:

_____

_____

_____

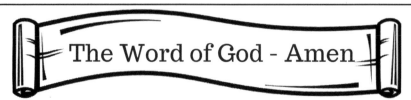

The Word of God - Amen

Date _____

Location _____

Sermon Title _____

Who's Preaching _____

Scripture _____

Word(s) To Look Up/Remember

_____

_____

Sermon Notes

_____

_____

_____

_____

_____

_____

_____

_____

_____

_____

_____

_____

_____

_____

_____

_____

_____

_____

_____

_____

_____

_____

_____

_____

_____

_____

_____

_____

_____

Today's sermon encourages me to:

_____

_____

_____

_____

A quote,saying I want to share:

_____

_____

_____

The Word of God - Amen

Date _____

Location _____

Sermon Title _____

Who's Preaching _____

Scripture _____

Word(s) To Look Up/Remember

_____

_____

Sermon Notes

_____

_____

_____

_____

_____

_____

_____

_____

_____

_____

_____

_____

_____

_____

_____

_____

_____

_____

_____

_____

_____

_____

_____

_____

_____

_____

_____

Today's sermon encourages me to:

_____

_____

_____

A quote,saying I want to share:

_____

_____

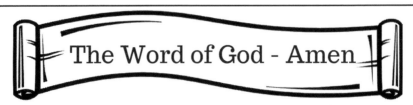

The Word of God - Amen

Date _____

Location _____

Sermon Title _____

Who's Preaching _____

Scripture _____

Word(s) To Look Up/Remember

_____

_____

Sermon Notes

_____

_____

_____

_____

_____

_____

_____

_____

_____

_____

_____

_____

_____

_____

_____

_____

_____

_____

_____

_____

_____

_____

_____

_____

_____

_____

_____

_____

Today's sermon encourages me to:

_____

_____

_____

A quote,saying I want to share:

_____

_____

_____

The Word of God - Amen

Date _____

Location _____

Sermon Title _____

Who's Preaching _____

Scripture _____

Word(s) To Look Up/Remember

_____

_____

Sermon Notes

_____

_____

_____

_____

_____

_____

_____

_____

_____

_____

_____

_____

_____

_____

_____

_____

_____

_____

_____

_____

_____

_____

_____

_____

_____

_____

_____

Today's sermon encourages me to:

_____

_____

_____

_____

A quote,saying I want to share:

_____

_____

_____

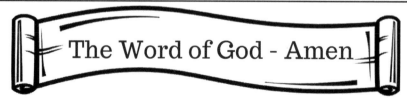

The Word of God - Amen

Date _____

Location _____

Sermon Title _____

Who's Preaching _____

Scripture _____

Word(s) To Look Up/Remember

_____

_____

Sermon Notes

_____

_____

_____

_____

_____

_____

_____

_____

_____

_____

_____

_____

_____

_____

_____

_____

_____

_____

_____

_____

_____

_____

_____

_____

_____

_____

_____

_____

Today's sermon encourages me to:

_____

_____

_____

_____

A quote,saying I want to share:

_____

_____

_____

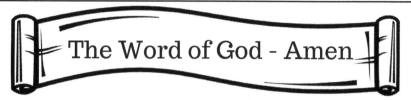

The Word of God - Amen

Date _____

Location _____

Sermon Title _____

Who's Preaching _____

Scripture _____

Word(s) To Look Up/Remember

_____

_____

Sermon Notes

_____

_____

_____

_____

_____

_____

_____

_____

_____

_____

_____

_____

_____

_____

_____

_____

_____

_____

_____

_____

_____

_____

_____

_____

_____

_____

_____

_____

_____

Today's sermon encourages me to:

_____

_____

_____

_____

A quote,saying I want to share:

_____

_____

_____

The Word of God - Amen

Date _____

Location _____

Sermon Title _____

Who's Preaching _____

Scripture _____

Word(s) To Look Up/Remember

_____

_____

Sermon Notes

_____

_____

_____

_____

_____

_____

_____

_____

_____

_____

_____

_____

_____

_____

_____

_____

_____

_____

_____

_____

_____

_____

_____

_____

_____

_____

_____

Today's sermon encourages me to:

_____

_____

_____

A quote, saying I want to share:

_____

_____

_____

The Word of God - Amen

Date _____

Location _____

Sermon Title _____

Who's Preaching _____

Scripture _____

Word(s) To Look Up/Remember

_____

_____

Sermon Notes

_____

_____

_____

_____

_____

_____

_____

_____

_____

_____

_____

_____

_____

_____

_____

_____

_____

_____

_____

_____

_____

_____

_____

_____

_____

_____

_____

_____

Today's sermon encourages me to:

_____

_____

_____

_____

A quote,saying I want to share:

_____

_____

_____

The Word of God - Amen

Date _____
Location _____
Sermon Title _____
Who's Preaching _____
Scripture _____

Word(s) To Look Up/Remember
_____
_____

Sermon Notes

_____
_____
_____
_____
_____
_____
_____
_____
_____
_____
_____
_____
_____
_____
_____
_____
_____
_____

_____

_____

_____

_____

_____

_____

_____

_____

_____

_____

_____

_____

Today's sermon encourages me to:

_____

_____

_____

_____

A quote,saying I want to share:

_____

_____

_____

The Word of God - Amen

Date _____

Location _____

Sermon Title _____

Who's Preaching _____

Scripture _____

Word(s) To Look Up/Remember

_____

_____

Sermon Notes

_____

_____

_____

_____

_____

_____

_____

_____

_____

_____

_____

_____

_____

_____

_____

_____

_____

_____

_____

_____

_____

_____

_____

_____

_____

_____

_____

_____

Today's sermon encourages me to:

_____

_____

_____

_____

A quote,saying I want to share:

_____

_____

_____

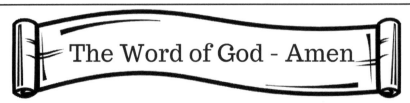

The Word of God - Amen

Date _____

Location _____

Sermon Title _____

Who's Preaching _____

Scripture _____

Word(s) To Look Up/Remember

_____

_____

Sermon Notes

_____

_____

_____

_____

_____

_____

_____

_____

_____

_____

_____

_____

_____

_____

_____

_____

_____

_____

_____

_____

_____

_____

_____

_____

_____

_____

_____

_____

_____

Today's sermon encourages me to:

_____

_____

_____

_____

A quote,saying I want to share:

_____

_____

_____

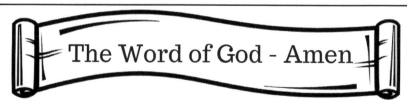

The Word of God - Amen

Date _____

Location _____

Sermon Title _____

Who's Preaching _____

Scripture _____

Word(s) To Look Up/Remember

_____

_____

Sermon Notes

_____

_____

_____

_____

_____

_____

_____

_____

_____

_____

_____

_____

_____

_____

_____

_____

_____

_____

_____

_____

_____

_____

_____

_____

_____

_____

_____

_____

Today's sermon encourages me to:

_____

_____

_____

A quote,saying I want to share:

_____

_____

_____

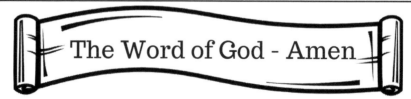

The Word of God - Amen

Date _____

Location _____

Sermon Title _____

Who's Preaching _____

Scripture _____

Word(s) To Look Up/Remember

_____

_____

Sermon Notes

_____

_____

_____

_____

_____

_____

_____

_____

_____

_____

_____

_____

_____

_____

_____

_____

_____

_____

_____

_____

_____

_____

_____

_____

_____

_____

_____

Today's sermon encourages me to:

_____

_____

_____

A quote,saying I want to share:

_____

_____

The Word of God - Amen

Date _____

Location _____

Sermon Title _____

Who's Preaching _____

Scripture _____

Word(s) To Look Up/Remember

_____

_____

Sermon Notes

_____

_____

_____

_____

_____

_____

_____

_____

_____

_____

_____

_____

_____

_____

_____

_____

_____

_____

_____

_____

_____

_____

_____

_____

_____

_____

_____

Today's sermon encourages me to:

_____

_____

_____

_____

A quote,saying I want to share:

_____

_____

_____

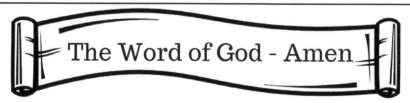

Date _____

Location _____

Sermon Title _____

Who's Preaching _____

Scripture _____

Word(s) To Look Up/Remember

_____

_____

Sermon Notes

Today's sermon encourages me to:

A quote,saying I want to share:

The Word of God - Amen

Date _____

Location _____

Sermon Title _____

Who's Preaching _____

Scripture _____

Word(s) To Look Up/Remember

_____

_____

Sermon Notes

_____

_____

_____

_____

_____

_____

_____

_____

_____

_____

_____

_____

_____

_____

_____

_____

_____

_____

_____

_____

_____

_____

_____

_____

_____

Today's sermon encourages me to:

_____

_____

_____

A quote, saying I want to share:

_____

_____

_____

The Word of God - Amen

Date _____

Location _____

Sermon Title _____

Who's Preaching _____

Scripture _____

Word(s) To Look Up/Remember

_____

_____

Sermon Notes

_____

_____

_____

_____

_____

_____

_____

_____

_____

_____

_____

_____

_____

_____

_____

_____

_____

_____

_____

_____

_____

_____

_____

_____

_____

_____

_____

Today's sermon encourages me to:

_____

_____

_____

_____

A quote,saying I want to share:

_____

_____

_____

The Word of God - Amen

Date _____

Location _____

Sermon Title _____

Who's Preaching _____

Scripture _____

Word(s) To Look Up/Remember

_____

_____

Sermon Notes

_____

_____

_____

_____

_____

_____

_____

_____

_____

_____

_____

_____

_____

_____

_____

_____

_____

_____

_____

_____

_____

_____

_____

_____

_____

_____

_____

_____

_____

Today's sermon encourages me to:

_____

_____

_____

A quote,saying I want to share:

_____

_____

_____

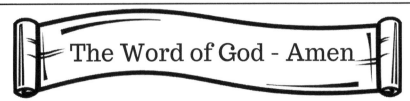

The Word of God - Amen

Date _____

Location _____

Sermon Title _____

Who's Preaching _____

Scripture _____

Word(s) To Look Up/Remember

_____

_____

Sermon Notes

_____

_____

_____

_____

_____

_____

_____

_____

_____

_____

_____

_____

_____

_____

_____

_____

_____

_____

_____

_____

_____

_____

_____

_____

_____

_____

Today's sermon encourages me to:

_____

_____

_____

_____

A quote,saying I want to share:

_____

_____

_____

The Word of God - Amen

Date _____

Location _____

Sermon Title _____

Who's Preaching _____

Scripture _____

Word(s) To Look Up/Remember

_____

_____

Sermon Notes

_____

_____

_____

_____

_____

_____

_____

_____

_____

_____

_____

_____

_____

_____

_____

_____

_____

_____

_____

_____

_____

_____

_____

_____

_____

_____

Today's sermon encourages me to:

_____

_____

_____

_____

A quote,saying I want to share:

_____

_____

_____

The Word of God - Amen

Date _____

Location _____

Sermon Title _____

Who's Preaching _____

Scripture _____

Word(s) To Look Up/Remember

_____

_____

Sermon Notes

_____

_____

_____

_____

_____

_____

_____

_____

_____

_____

_____

_____

_____

_____

_____

_____

_____

_____

_____

_____

_____

_____

_____

_____

_____

_____

_____

_____

_____

_____

Today's sermon encourages me to:

_____

_____

_____

_____

A quote,saying I want to share:

_____

_____

_____

The Word of God - Amen

Date _____

Location _____

Sermon Title _____

Who's Preaching _____

Scripture _____

Word(s) To Look Up/Remember

_____

_____

Sermon Notes

_____

_____

_____

_____

_____

_____

_____

_____

_____

_____

_____

_____

_____

_____

_____

_____

_____

_____

_____

_____

_____

_____

_____

_____

_____

_____

_____

Today's sermon encourages me to:

_____

_____

_____

_____

A quote,saying I want to share:

_____

_____

_____

The Word of God - Amen

Date _____

Location _____

Sermon Title _____

Who's Preaching _____

Scripture _____

Word(s) To Look Up/Remember

_____

_____

Sermon Notes

_____

_____

_____

_____

_____

_____

_____

_____

_____

_____

_____

_____

_____

_____

_____

_____

_____

_____

_____

_____

_____

_____

_____

_____

_____

_____

_____

_____

Today's sermon encourages me to:

_____

_____

_____

_____

A quote,saying I want to share:

_____

_____

_____

The Word of God - Amen

Date _____

Location _____

Sermon Title _____

Who's Preaching _____

Scripture _____

Word(s) To Look Up/Remember

_____

_____

Sermon Notes

_____

_____

_____

_____

_____

_____

_____

_____

_____

_____

_____

_____

_____

_____

_____

_____

_____

_____

_____

_____

_____

_____

_____

_____

_____

_____

Today's sermon encourages me to:

_____

_____

_____

_____

A quote, saying I want to share:

_____

_____

_____

The Word of God - Amen

Date _____
Location _____
Sermon Title _____
Who's Preaching _____
Scripture _____

Word(s) To Look Up/Remember

_____

_____

Sermon Notes

_____
_____
_____
_____
_____
_____
_____
_____
_____
_____
_____
_____
_____
_____
_____
_____
_____

_____

_____

_____

_____

_____

_____

_____

_____

_____

_____

_____

Today's sermon encourages me to:

_____

_____

_____

A quote,saying I want to share:

_____

_____

_____

The Word of God - Amen

Made in the USA
Middletown, DE
15 June 2022

67186265R00075